THE PATIENT GLORIA

Gina Moxley

THE PATIENT GLORIA

OBERON BOOKS
LONDON

WWW.OBERONBOOKS.COM

First published in 2019 by Oberon Books Ltd
521 Caledonian Road, London N7 9RH
Tel: +44 (0) 20 7607 3637 / Fax: +44 (0) 20 7607 3629
e-mail: info@oberonbooks.com
www.oberonbooks.com

PB ISBN: 9781786828316
E ISBN: 9781786828330

Series: Oberon Modern Plays

Cover image by Luca Truffarelli

eBook conversion by Lapiz Digital Services, India.

Presented by Gina Moxley and the Abbey Theatre in association with Pan Pan Theatre Company, *The Patient Gloria* was first performed at the Abbey Theatre, Dublin on 28 September 2018 as part of Dublin Theatre Festival, with the following cast and creatives:

CAST	Gina Moxley
	Liv O'Donoghue
Musician	Zoe Ní Riordáin
Writer	Gina Moxley
Director	John McIlduff
Choreographer	Liv O'Donoghue
Set Design	Andrew Clancy
Costume Design	Sarah Bacon
Sound Design	Adam Welsh
Lighting Design	Sinéad Wallace
AV Design	Conan McIvor
Stage Manager	Fiona Keller
Production Manager	Anthony Hanley
Producer	Aoife White
Photographer	Luca Truffarelli

It received its UK premiere at the Traverse Theatre, Edinburgh on 1 August 2019 with Jane Deasy as musician.

Characters

GINA plays herself and DR ROGERS,
DR PERLS and DR ELLIS

LIV plays GLORIA

JANE plays bass guitar

The voice of SHOSTROM is played
through speakers

Part I

The set includes a therapist's couch, chair, plants, coffee table. Cool, mid-century vibe. A chair for GLORIA and a table for mic and ashtray.

GINA is sewing at GLORIA's table as the audience enter. LIV is draped across the couch. On clearance…

GINA: Can you see me? That any better? Can you see me now? You can? Wow. Yes. Miraculous. You should not be able to see me at all. Seriously, I've been fading for years and am technically invisible by now. Recently, I got on a completely empty bus, first person on it, and then a man got on at the next stop and sat on me, didn't see me at all. That's how invisible I am. Ancient. But you can see me. Odd. Oh. Right. Maybe it's the shirt and tie? Huh? Ah. Or the dick? Is it this? That's what you see, is it? Listen, it is as much a surprise to me as it is to you to find myself here making a dick. Sewing. I'm about to play three men – yeah, because I want to – so I felt I needed to get a true feeling for the apparent sense of authority and entitlement that comes with this lump of meat, of manhood. Since I've always been good with my hands I thought I'd make myself a nice, muscular dick to help me get into character. For some people it's the shoes, in this case I need a bit of anatomy. This dotie dick here I made from memory, well, memories – cumulative. It's just tights stuffed with cotton wool and some bird seed – for gravity, gravitas.

And a bit of an elbow patch from an old cardi there for the scrotum. It's actually in danger of turning into our President Michael D. Higgins. Wuzza wuzza wuzza little Miggledy Dickeldy. I mean that with the greatest respect by the way. It is Presidential. Wow. Whoa, the heat, the power. There's no controlling this beast. Now I get it. Now I understand corruption, porn, cycling. Only kidding. Snowballs. Lookit, women's sexual organs are so hidden we don't even realise ourselves what's going on half the time. We didn't even have a name for down there when we were growing up. But in a lie detector test it transpires that we are turned on by way way way more than we would ever otherwise admit to. Isn't that right Liv? Sorry, this is Liv O'Donoghue by the way. Liv will be playing Gloria. Liv? LIV? Actually, she already is Gloria. Yes, I can promise you every other woman here is pulsing with rampant desire this very minute. Can you hear it?

Music – operated by GINA *hitting a pedal.*

Jesus, the deafening *thrummmmm* of unbridled, slithery carnality, of boldness, of smartness and couldn't-give-a-fuck-ness. Can you smell it? Oh ho ho my sisters. I know what's going on with you lot.

LIV/GLORIA comes downstage. JANE comes onto the stage.

Oh it's getting hot in here. When we were making this show we felt a responsibility to show the infinite variety of women, we thought we needed a role model with us, like a dominatrix or an orthodontist, maybe a dog groomer. Nah, then we thought we'd represent females of different ages. So we thought about having a child in the show but you know what? Between police clearance, chaperones and my ambivalence about motherhood we thought fuck that, give us a rock 'n' roll model instead. Yeah, so here's the fabulous Jane Deasy. Go Jane, you be you. Do be doo. Let it out. Rip it up. Get it on.

JANE rips into 'Shitlist' by L7.

GINA and GLORIA dance.

AV title: 'The Patient Gloria'.

GINA on the couch. GLORIA at her table on mic.

GLORIA: California, 1964. Love has vacated my life. I pack my three kids in the car and head west. After a lot of broken crockery – guilty – I leave my husband, marriage and the Catholic Church. I'm a single woman. Thirty. Flirty. Chain-smoking. Broke and horny. I get a job as a waitress. Working for tips. I'm in therapy with Dr Everett Shostrom. He has the idea to make some teaching films with three eminent psychotherapists for use in psychology classes in schools and colleges all over the country. He asks me to be the actual patient engaged in therapy on screen 'before your very eyes'. The poster girl for psychotherapy! I thought, sure, Gloria, you can do this. You know this shit. Pardon my French. And I have to admit, I really liked smart men. A lot. Guilty.

The crew were really kind to me, like I was some kind of star. Heck, I was, I had to go through that three times. I'd seen the set earlier, looked so real, just like a therapist's office. First I was meeting the very famous Dr Carl Rogers, author of *On Becoming a Person*. I guess that's what I wanted, to be more me. Happy with me. Learn to live with myself. Wasn't it? He was like the godfather of counselling. He didn't know it yet but he would be nominated for a Nobel Peace Prize years from then.

She moves away from the table and mic. Gets ready for therapy.

Is it hot in here? Alrighty then, got my problem all prepared. Ready for guidance. Solutions. Get rid of some goddamn guilt.

AV title: 'Three Approaches to Psychotherapy'.

SCENE 2

Every time SHOSTROM *speaks,* GLORIA *and* GINA *face an offstage monitor.*

SHOSTROM: *(Voiceover.)* Psychotherapy is such a personal and private process that it is a mystery to most people who have never gone through it. The following series is a unique effort that allows us to sit in on what is ordinarily a very private therapeutic experience. An actual patient was courageous and considerate enough to allow herself to be photographed while actually engaging in therapy with three different therapists. A film like this, with three therapists distinguished by their different orientations, has never been made before. The series will be divided into three separate films. In the first film we see Dr Carl Rogers, founder of Person-Centred Therapy, interviewing Gloria.

GINA places the dick on the chest of drawers.

SHOSTROM: *(Voiceover.)* Now, here's Dr Carl Rogers.

AV title: 'Therapy Session 1'.

ROGERS: Good morning.

GLORIA: Hello, Dr Rogers.

ROGERS: I'm Dr Rogers, you must be Gloria. *(They shake hands. She sits.)*

GLORIA: Yes, I am.

ROGERS: Won't you have a seat? *(Breathing.)* Now then, we don't have much time together, and I really don't know what we will be able to make of it but, uh, I hope we can make something of it. I'd be glad to know *(breathing)* whatever concerns you.

JANE: He's hyperventilating. Of course he is, it's the artificiality of the situation.

GINA: The high from that dick more like.

JANE: The heat of the lights. The outside situation.

GINA: Is the breathing too much?

JANE: Yeah, it's distracting. Start again…

Reset.

ROGERS: Good morning.

GLORIA: Hello, Dr Rogers.

ROGERS: I'm Dr Rogers. You must be Gloria. *(They shake hands. She sits.)*

GLORIA: Yesssss. Yes I am.

ROGERS: Won't you have a seat? We don't have much time together, I hope we'll get something out of it. Can you tell me what concerns you?

GLORIA: Well, right now I'm nervous – talking about my private life in front of everybody. It's…

ROGERS: I can hear the tremor in your voice so I know you are…

GLORIA: Uh well, I'm just newly divorced, I've been in therapy before… My biggest problem is adjusting to my single life. Uh, men essentially. Having sex with men other than…

ROGERS: Mhmmm-hmmm.

GLORIA: Having uh men, men coming to the house. And how it affects the children. I've been making love for eleven years…

ROGERS: Mhmmm-hmmm. *(Laugh.)*

GLORIA: Not consistently of course. Not non-stop for eleven years. Quite a lot though. You know what I mean. And the main thing I want, what I want to talk about, tell you about is, uh, I have a daughter, Pammy, nine, who has some emotional problems due to the divorce, and I'm afraid she must've snuck into my room or something when a man was present and we were making love – well, having sex, I'm not sure it was love if I'm honest, or she saw or heard me with… I wish I could stop shaking. Look at me. Shaking. I wish I could just stop with the shaking.

Sound of a plane overhead. He looks up at the plane. She comes. He misses it.

I'm real conscious of things upsetting her. Uh, I don't want her to be upset. To shock her. I want so bad for

7

her to accept me. We're real open with each other, especially about sex… She's always been curious about it, I caught her stealing a sex manual I had in my bureau a few years ago. I was open with her. Told her it's natural.

ROGERS: Nine, you say. Mhmmm-hmmm.

JANE: Yes, nine.

GLORIA: The other day she asked, 'Mommy, did you ever go to bed with anyone besides daddy?' And I lied to her. I looked straight into her eyes and lied. 'No, honey.' I mean, what was I meant to say? 'Sure honey everyone does.' Oh shit. It keeps coming into my mind. I feel so guilty having lied to her. I never lie, I hate liars. I want… I can't help wanting… I remember when I was a little girl and found out my parents made love, oh, it was dirty, terrible. I was particularly disgusted by my Mom. I know it's dumb. I don't want to lie to Pammy. I want her to trust me. How would she feel if I told her the truth – sure honey, I've slept with a lot of men since I left your daddy. I'm not the good Mommy you thought I was. Is that so wrong? I want, I want, I want you to tell me, I want an answer from you.

ROGERS: I sure wish I could give you the answer as to what you should do.

GLORIA: If she believed me she will think I'm so good and goddamn sweet that she can't open up, but if she thinks I lied then she knows I am a devil. A dirty devil.

ROGERS: If she really knew you would she, could she, accept you?

GLORIA: Yes, that's what I said. Are you going to repeat what I said back to me all through this session, is that it? I want more. I want you to help me get rid of my guilt about lying or fucking single men. I want to be able to act on my desires but I feel so guilty.

ROGERS: This is a private thing I couldn't possibly answer for you but I'm sure as anything the answer is within you.

GLORIA: You know doctor, sure I really try to be a good mother but it is so lonely and boring. And when I have these raging physical desires for some casual man, I'll say, 'Oh shoot, why not? Because you really want it bad Gloria.' And afterwards the guilt comes in. But I can't stop the desires. I tried saying, 'Gloria you don't like yourself when you do this so stop.' And then I resent the children. I want it. So I do it. Is it all that bad? To just have sex because you're physically attracted?

ROGERS: You feel you're not acting in accord with your own inner standards, that you can't help that… uh…either.

GLORIA: That's it. I can't control myself and now I feel like a devil. There are too many things I do wrong that I have to feel guilty for. I don't like that. I hate the guilt. Help me. Give me a direct answer. If I'm open and honest with my children will it harm them? Will they

hate me? Will it bother them more? I want to get rid
of my guilt. But I don't want to put it on Pammy.
Guilt kills.

GINA: Guilt kills.

JANE: Guilt kills. Ain't that the truth. Go on, I'll back you
up here.

JANE plays.

GINA: Cork, 1964. This was at a time when manners were
more important than anything else. The glory days of
domestic violence, drunken driving, child abuse and
cockeyed Catholicism. Last time I was at the Flynn's
had been with my grandmother, she had a heart attack
and shat in their bed. First time I'd ever seen her lose
control. Or any woman lose control actually. Now it
was a birthday party for the Flynns' daughter. I was
wearing a dress my mother made and my communion
shoes. Scuffed, no longer white. Dropped at the gate,
I was given the drill – do what you're told. Say please.
Say thank you. Eat whatever you're offered, even if
you don't want it, even if you don't like it. Don't speak
with your mouth full. Wash your hands after you use
the bathroom. No rooting in drawers or poking around.
Talk to the other girls. Play. Join in. Help. Be nice.
Be good. Smile.

What was the point? I was damned already. Branded
by original sin. Guilty. God, surrounded by cushions,
twirling his moustache and pointing from his smug

fucking perch up above, picked me out as I walked alone up the path to the door and occasions of sin. He could see through my pink dress and vest to my soul – wherever that was – blackened with ancestral fault. Weakened and diminished by Adam's fall, I was ushered into a room filled with sandwiches and iced gems, butterfly buns and Krispie cakes. Balloons. Cards. Tiers of food endlessly offered. Candles blazing and sweet girls singing. A choir of Eves. The bad angel apple trees out the back scratching at the window, screaming temptation. The scabby fruits of sin dangling as if it was nothing to do with them. I am just an apple; don't bother trying to blame me. None of the other girls seemed a bit perturbed. They were probably just used to being rotten. Another sandwich? Giving me the gawks. Cake, a slice, go on. Buns? Stacking up in my throat. My waistband digging into me. My fingers pudging up. Musical chairs. More food. Pass the parcel. And more plates. Not allowed to say no. Rude to say no. Good girls don't say no. Committing a capital sin out of politeness. Gluttony. You pig, you glutton, God sneered as I waddled to my mother's car. Pointing, sparks coming out of his fingers at me. Zig-zags of lightning. So, so disappointed in you. You glutton. Glutton girl. You'll pay for this. Forever.

I knelt in the dark, full to the throat, full as a tick, bursting out of my skin. My nightie hurting. Kneeling. Praying. Crying. Riddled with guilt. Trying to explain my dilemma. But heaven was dark, God was asleep. Nubbins of horns under my hair. I would not vomit.

Was waste a worse sin than gluttony? I am guilty. I am weak and prone to temptation. Hell is calling. I am bad. Guilty. Rotten to my apple core. Oh my God, I am heartily sorry for having offended thee. I detest my sins as much as egg sandwiches. I am seven.

Years later a French girl…

JANE: Odille. Her name was Odille.

GINA: Yes, Odille told me about evolution. And what that forbidden fruit bullshit was really about. Sex! I felt so stupid. Okay, the apple was a bit far-fetched but seriously Odille, are you trying to tell me we come from a fish?

GLORIA is lying on the floor, eating an apple.

GLORIA: Do you feel that could hurt her?

She joins ROGERS downstage.

ROGERS: One thing I might ask, what is it you wish I would say to you?

GLORIA: I wish you'd say be honest and take the risk that Pammy's going to accept you. If she knows what a demon I am and still loves me then maybe I can accept myself more. Like it's not really that bad.

ROGERS takes the apple and puts it on the table.

ROGERS: So yeah, you want her to see what a devil you can be and that you do things she might not approve of, that you don't always approve of, but that she'd somehow love you and accept you as an imperfect person.

GLORIA: Yes, I want Pammy to accept me as a full woman.

ROGERS returns stage left of GLORIA.

ROGERS: You don't sound so uncertain. I guess one thing I feel very keenly is that – it's an awful risky thing to live.

GLORIA: I uh – *(Sighs, eyes welling up.)* I do feel like you're saying, not giving me advice but saying you really wanna…you know what you want Gloria, just go right ahead and do it. I sort of feel you're backing me up.

ROGERS: Uh, you've been telling me that you know what you want to do and yes, I believe in backing people up. You know more about you than anyone else ever will. You feel whole, all in one piece.

GLORIA: Gives me a choked up feeling. I don't get that as often as I'd like. I like that whole feeling. That's real precious to me.

GLORIA gets teary again. ROGERS gets her a tissue.

ROGERS: I expect none of us gets it as often as we'd like, but I really do understand it. Mhmmm, that really does touch you, doesn't it?

GLORIA: I feel dumb saying this but while you were talking I was thinking gee, how nice I can talk to you and I want you to approve of me and I respect you. I miss that my father couldn't talk to me like you do.

GINA: *(To JANE.)* Is he a therapist?

JANE: No, he has a chemical company.

GLORIA and ROGERS face each other.

GLORIA: I mean, I'd like to say, 'Gee, I'd like you for a father.'

ROGERS: …Mhmm-hmmmm.

GLORIA: I don't know where that came from.

ROGERS: You look to me like a pretty nice daughter.

GLORIA: That's why I like substitutes. Men I can talk to and respect. Like doctors. You know? Underneath there's a feeling like we're real close. Like uh, a substitute father.

ROGERS walks backwards, then moves the couch downstage behind GLORIA.

ROGERS: I don't feel that's pretending.

GLORIA: Well, you're not really my father.

ROGERS: No. I meant about the close business.

GLORIA: How can you feel close to me? You don't know me.

ROGERS: Well, I…just feel close to you in this moment.

He spreads GLORIA's legs. Agitated, transfixed by her crotch.

GLORIA: Well okay. I'd just want more of it I guess.

ROGERS: *(Pointing at her vulva.)* Is that a big need? Would it take a lot of love and understanding to fill it up?

GLORIA: I've been so busy trying to get rid of my neurosis. I'd like to just find someone who will love me like a father. I want this in boyfriends. I want an older man that's caring and mature and not so flip.

ROGERS: You really want to find a father who'll love and accept you the way you are.

GLORIA: Yes. Since I left my husband the only men I go out with are the kind I don't respect, the young, flip, not caring, smart-aleck kind of guy. Not somebody that's…you know, respectable. That's a big thing.

ROGERS: *(Voiceover as he dives between her legs. Voice muffled.)* So you're slapping your father in the face, aren't you?

ROGERS wriggles up under her skirt, as if disappearing into her.

GLORIA: Oh? By wanting mature men?

ROGERS: *(Voiceover.)* No. By going out with those who are quite unlike the ones you really want.

Unseen, ROGERS exits through the back of the couch.

GLORIA: But I told you. I don't mean to. I don't understand why they keep coming round.

SCENE 3
POST-THERAPY

GLORIA to mic.

GLORIA: I am in motion
Moving forward
Not just who I hoped to be
Or should be
But actually me.
Guilt kills.

ROGERS re-appears from the back of the couch. Recovers with difficulty. Glasses askew.

ROGERS: In the best moments of therapy there is a mutual altered state of consciousness…we really, both of us, somehow transcend a little bit of what we are ordinarily, there is communication going on that neither of us understands. I guess I feel good about myself in the interview, and like Gloria I feel very real regret that the relationship cannot continue.

GLORIA: But it will, Dr Rogers. You and your wife will become my ghost parents. We will write letters to each other until the end. Through my marriage, my training to be a nurse, my son's death. You will say I can call you anytime. I have yet to learn that there is so much living in dying. Sometime in the far future Pammy and I will drive by your house. Round and round all afternoon. I will have your home phone number on a slip of paper. We will find a payphone. I will not have the nerve to call.

JANE: Dr Rogers gave advice five times. Asked three questions. Used 'encouragers' five times. He spoke thirty per cent of the time and Gloria spoke 5,508 words or seventy per cent of the time. He moved house so often as a child he was never able to establish friendships. His own early trauma manifests in him wanting to maintain a relationship with Gloria.

GINA: I was avuncular. Too wholesome. Flaccid. It needed a bit more of a poke. I should've worn the dick. Doctor Emptypants.

JANE: Paternal. You were paternal. And all that carries.

GINA: Ah, cheers Jane.

AV: Flower interlude.

GINA looks at the flower projection, traces the stamens.

GLORIA: 'He says he has a beautiful view from his house,' I will tell Pammy. 'He has lots of roses. And geraniums and lilies and chrysanthemums and asters. Can you imagine that? Roses. He tends roses.'

Part II

JANE plays. GLORIA does her nails and moans at the table mic downstage right.

GINA: Yeah. This makes me think about dicks. Hard not to really. They're everywhere aren't they? The ubiquitous dick. Walking down the street is an assault course of dicks. A cock guard of honour. People being dicks and actual dicks. Quite partial to a few of them over the years.

She takes a pink, limp, fake penis from the drawer.

Is this a trigger dick? Sorry if it is upsetting. I should've asked. But to be honest, it didn't occur to me. All I was aware of was it. My dick. My damn fine big swinging dick.

The world is awash with unasked-for dicks. I have a lifetime of dicks I never asked to see. I saw the first dick I didn't ask to see on a bus. I was about eight. This guy unzipped for us kids. Somehow I was given a kitten at the same time. Pussy in a box.

JANE: Dick on the bus.

GINA: The dick I put my hand on by mistake in the cinema. Or was put into my hand I should say. I was around eleven. These guys ranged around in the dark trying to trick girls into touching them. Many is the movie ruined.

JANE: Dick at the Ritz.

GINA: A friend of my father's, drunk, on the payphone in our pub. Pissing into a fruit bowl. His dick flapping like a flag.

JANE: Dinosaur dick.

GINA: The fella who flashed at us kids in our swimsuits from across the river. Clownish check jacket, made sure we saw him alright.

JANE: Bozo the Dick.

GINA: At school we had three after class options – tennis, smoking or looking at Mr Prick. Over the wall at the end of the grounds. Four twenty-five on the dot. Wanking pathetically.

JANE: Dick at recreation.

GINA: The doctor who gave me a spin in his sports car, flicking his dick at me. The teeth of the zip biting into him. Sore-looking.

JANE: Dr Dick On Call.

GINA: The guy in a GAA shirt, pushed me into a doorway. Got his stumpy dick out. Hoofed him in the balls.

JANE: Back-of-the-net Dick.

GINA: The teenager wanking next to me by a pool in Wiesbaden, Germany. Where Elvis met Priscilla and Dostoevsky lost a fortune.

JANE: Der Dangling Dick.

GINA: The naked man in the window after I left the hospital where my stepfather was dying. Wanking, waiting for a passer-by.

JANE: Depressed Dick.

GINA: And on and on ad infinitum. It's okay lads we have seen your fucking dicks now put them away. But no.

JANE: They tried to stop us walking alone in the dark. Stop hitchhiking. Stop going for swims on our own.

GINA: Nevertheless we persisted.

JANE: Our lives proscribed by dicks. One hand on your shoulder shoving you down regardless of what you'd like. Sure we've even forgotten ourselves.

GINA: Our mouths the most acceptable orifice. As soon as they learn to suck their own fucking dicks and cut the woman out of the spit-roasts and fuck each other, the better.

ALL THREE: We'll see ourselves out. Thanks!

GINA: Was that a bit much?

JANE: They're only the edited highlights of the catalogue.

GINA: Of the analogue catalogue. We had the real thing but it's all gone digital now. Dick pics. Did you ever want to have a dick, Jane?

JANE: For myself like? No. Handy for opening doors I suppose.

GINA: I'm actually giving myself a stiffie here. So, this is my next character's dick. Fritz Perls' big swinging dick. I'll give you therapy. Using it during that dickologue was completely gratuitous. I'll tuck it in 'cause I'm putting myself off my stroke here with this sort of showing off. So easy to fall into. So hard to let it go.

GINA tucks the dick into her trousers. They all face the monitor offstage.

SCENE 2

SHOSTROM: *(Voiceover.)* Psychotherapy is sometimes described as a process of helping a person to help himself. First you've seen Dr Carl Rogers, founder of Client-Centred Therapy, at work with our real live patient. Now we invite you to observe Dr Frederick Perls, founder of Gestalt therapy, with the same patient.

JANE: Hang on, founder of Gestalt therapy – with his wife Laura.

GLORIA at mic. PERLS sits.

GLORIA: I caught sight of him earlier. He's like a cross between Santa Claus and Rasputin. Attractive and repulsive. He's both, simultaneously. Oh, I shouldn't get hung up on his demeanour. He makes me anxious already. So damn smart. And the producer's favourite. In fact Dr Shostrom has been in therapy with Dr Perls.

JANE: Frame violation. Professional boundaries are components that constitute the therapeutic frame. They represent the limit of the appropriate behaviour by the psychotherapist in the clinical setting. Any deviations from this can be called frame violations, great name for a band, by the way. 'Every major trauma involves some kind of frame violation, while every frame violation is a traumatic experience.'

GLORIA: Frame violation was the least of it, it was such a betrayal.

SHOSTROM: *(Voiceover.)* Dr Frederick Perls.

AV title: 'Therapy Session 2'.

PERLS addresses the audience. GLORIA starts to circle the couch.

PERLS: I am to interview a patient and I'd like to give
you some thumbnail sketch of what Gestalt therapy
stands for.

JANE: The word Gestalt means whole. With a W.

PERLS: A Gestalt therapist tries to focus on what is
happening in the moment and on finding solutions in
the present time. Once the patient has learned to stand
on his own feet, his need for therapy will collapse.
He will wake up from the nightmare of his existence.
I disregard most of the content of what the patient says
and concentrate most on the non-verbal level, as this is
the only one which is less subject to self-deception.

SCENE 3

PERLS: We are going to have an interview for half an hour.

GLORIA: Right away I'm scared.

PERLS: You say you're scared, but you're smiling.
A frightened person does not smile. Well, do you have
stage fright.

GLORIA: I'm afraid you're going to have such a direct
attack that you're going to get me in a corner.

She puts her hand to her throat. He mimics her.

PERLS: Is this your corner?

GLORIA: It's like I'm afraid, you know.

PERLS: Can you describe the corner you'd like to go to?

GLORIA: Yeah, ah, it's back in the corner.

PERLS: There you would be safe from me. What would
you do in that corner?

GLORIA: I'd just sit.

PERLS: Just sit?

GLORIA: Yes. When I was a little girl, every time I was
afraid, I'd feel better sitting in a corner.

PERLS: Are you a little girl?

GLORIA: Well no, but it's the same feeling.

PERLS: Are you a little girl?

GLORIA: This feeling reminds me of it.

PERLS: Are you a little girl?

GLORIA: No, no, no.

PERLS: No, at last. How old are you?

GLORIA: Thirty.

PERLS: Then you're not a little girl.

GLORIA: No.

PERLS: Okay. So you're a thirty-year-old girl who's afraid of a guy like me. Now, what can I do to you?

GLORIA: You can't do anything, but I can sure feel dumb, and I can feel stupid for not having the right answers. I hate it when I'm stupid.

PERLS: What would it do for you to be dumb and stupid? What would it do to me if you would play dumb and stupid?

GLORIA: It makes you all the smarter and all the higher above me. Then I really have to look up to you, 'cause you're so smart, yeah.

PERLS: Oh, oh yeah, butter me up right and left.

GLORIA: No, I think you can do that all by yourself.

PERLS: Ah, if you play dumb and stupid, you force me to be more explicit.

GLORIA: That's been said to me before, but I don't really – I don't buy it.

PERLS: What are you doing with your feet now?

GLORIA: *(Laughing.)* Wiggling them.

PERLS: What's the joke now?

GLORIA: You're treating me as if I'm stronger than I am and I want you to protect me more and be nicer to me.

PERLS: You don't believe a word what you're saying.

GLORIA: I do too and I know you're going to pick on me for it.

PERLS: Sure, you're a bluff, you're a phony.

GLORIA: You're meaning that seriously?

PERLS: Yeah, if you say you're afraid and you laugh and giggle and you squirm, that's phony. You put on a performance for me.

GLORIA: Oh, I… I resent that very much.

PERLS: Can you express this?

GLORIA: Yes, sir, I most certainly am not being phony. I will admit this. It's hard for me to show my embarrassment, I hate to be embarrassed. But boy I resent you calling me a phony. Just because I smile when I'm embarrassed or I'm put in a corner, doesn't mean I'm being a phony.

PERLS: *(Offers his hand.)* Wonderful, thank you. You didn't smile for the last minute.

GLORIA: Well, I'm mad at you. I…

PERLS: Now that you're mad you're not a phony.

GLORIA: I still resent that, I'm not a phony when I'm nervous. *(Hits couch.)*

PERLS: *(Mimics her.)* Again. Again. Again.

GLORIA: I want to get mad at you. I, I, I… You know what I want to do?

PERLS: I, I, I, I – *(Kicking his feet in the air.)*

GLORIA: I want you on my level. So I can pick on you, just as much as you're picking on me.

PERLS: Okay, pick on me. *(Stands on the couch, gestures with both hands.)*

GLORIA: I have to wait till you say something that I can pick on, but – *(Both whirling hands.)*

PERLS: What does this mean? Can you develop this movement? *(Both gesture.)*

GLORIA: It's a, I can't find words. I want to…

PERLS: Develop this, as if you were dancing.

GLORIA: I want to start all over again with you.

PERLS: Okay, let's start all over.

PERLS sits back in his chair; GLORIA moves to the couch.

GLORIA: I have a feeling you don't like me right off the bat and I want to know if you do.

PERLS: Play Fritz Perls not liking Gloria? What would he say?

GLORIA: He'd say that she's a phony, for one.

PERLS: Say you are a phony.

GLORIA: You're a phony, and you're a flip little girl, and you're a show-off.

PERLS: What would Gloria answer to that?

GLORIA: I, I, I know what I'd answer. I'd say I think you are too.

PERLS: Now say, tell this to me. Tell me what a phony I am. Say: 'Fritz you're a phony.'

GLORIA: Well, phony is not quite the right word, but it's more like a show-off.

PERLS: A show-off?

GLORIA: Like you know all the answers. And I want you to be more human.

PERLS: To know all the answers is not very human?

GLORIA: Yeah, to right away find out how I'm kicking my feet and why am I doing like this. *(Gestures with her arms.)* Why are you doing like that?

PERLS: Oh dear, I've got eyes and I can see you're kicking your feet.

GLORIA: Okay. I'd like you to accept it, instead of putting me on the defensive having to explain it. I don't want to have to explain why I'm doing these things.

PERLS: Did I ask you to explain it?

GLORIA sighs.

Now do this again.

GLORIA sighs.

Again.

GLORIA sighs.

He orchestrates her sighs to a frantic pitch.

PERLS: How do you feel now?

GLORIA: I don't know.

PERLS: Playing stupid?

PERLS goes to his chair and faces away from her.

GLORIA: I'm not playing stupid, I don't know the right answer.

PERLS: You say I don't know, this is playing stupid…
You did something with your hair there. Is there by any chance something with my hair which you object to?

GLORIA: No but, I…your hair and your features go along with the, the feeling I had about you earlier. You're the type of person that seems like you demand so much respect and so…

PERLS: Please play Fritz, I demand so much respect. Play this Fritz you just saw.

GLORIA: Well, you know how smart I am. I know more about psychology than you do, Gloria. So anything I say of course is right.

PERLS: Can you say the same as Gloria? With the same act as Gloria? I demand respect because…

GLORIA: I don't feel I demand respect.

PERLS: You don't demand respect?

GLORIA: As a matter of fact, I'd like more.

They circle the couch.

PERLS: Now you see, so you do demand respect.

GLORIA: If I could demand respect from you I would.

PERLS: Now do it. Who's preventing you, except yourself?

GLORIA: 'Cause I feel if I get myself out of the corner, you're going to let me just…drown. You're not going to help me.

She drops to the floor, hiding her face.

PERLS: What should I do when you're in the corner?

GLORIA: Encourage me to come out.

He joins her on the floor.

PERLS: Ah. You don't have enough courage to come out by yourself? You need someone to pull little mademoiselle in distress out of her corner.

GLORIA: Yes.

PERLS: So any time you want somebody to uh, pay attention to you, you crawl into a corner and wait till the rescuer comes.

GLORIA: Yes, that's exactly what I'd like.

PERLS: And this is what I call phony.

GLORIA: Pardon me?

PERLS: This is what I call phony.

GLORIA: Why is it phony? I'm admitting to you what I am. How is that a phony?

PERLS: That is a phony, because it's a trick, a gimmick, to crawl into a corner and wait there until somebody comes to your rescue.

GLORIA: I know what I'm doing. I'm not being phony; I'm not pretending I'm so brave. I resent that. I feel like you're saying unless I come out, openly and stand on my own, I'm a phony. Baloney, I'm just as real sitting in that corner as I am out here all by myself.

PERLS: But you're not sitting in that corner.

GLORIA: Well, not now. You feel so secure you don't have to feel. Well, I resent it. I feel you're playing one big game.

PERLS: Sure, we're playing games, but I think I hit the bullseye when I called you phony. That's why you feel hurt.

GLORIA: I don't know, all I know is when I feel the way I feel with you right now, I, I – it's like you don't have feeling.

She gestures and he imitates her.

PERLS: Now exaggerate this, what you just did. That's it; now talk to me like this.

GLORIA: I can't. I can't. I want to laugh. I want… I'd like you to be younger than me, so I could really scold you.

PERLS: Imagine that I'm thirty, and now you scold me.

GLORIA: Okay, don't be so cocksure of yourself. Don't think you're so doggone smart. Don't act so proud because you've never been in the corner. I think you can be just as big a phony. Parading around like you're so damn smart and you know all the answers, as much as me sitting in my corner. Oh, and I like the feeling of you being younger. I'd like to really, I'd like to embarrass you.

PERLS: Tell me, embarrass me. Tell me how old, how ugly I am.

GLORIA: You don't look old and ugly. You look distinguished, and that gives you, that's all the more on your side if you look so distinguished then.

PERLS: Well Gloria, can we say one thing? We had quite a good fight.

GLORIA: No, ah, no. Mm-mm, I don't think you're fighting with me.

PERLS: But…you came out quite a bit.

GLORIA: Well, I'm mad at you.

PERLS: Wonderful.

GLORIA lies down on the couch. He joins her, sitting on the edge.

GLORIA: I feel like you're not recognizing me at all,
Dr Perls, not a bit.

PERLS: Our contact is much too superficial to be involved
in caring. I respect you so much as a human being
that I refuse to accept the phony part of yourself and
address myself only to the genuine part. Right now,
the last few minutes you were wonderfully genuine.
You weren't playing anymore. I could see you were
really hurting.

GLORIA: Well, I don't feel I've got a right when I disagree
with what somebody's doing, if I should respect them
if they're superior to me. I don't feel I have a right to
really, really tell you how mad I am at you.

PERLS: That's, that's, that's garbage. You're now jackety-
jacketing, you're getting back into your safe corner.

GLORIA jumps up away from him. He follows. They circle the couch.

PERLS: Quack quack quack quack quack quack quack
quack. You came out for a moment. You nearly met
me, could get a little bit angry with me. Now go back to
your safety.

GLORIA: I'd be scared to death to cry in front of you.

PERLS: You mustn't cry in my presence.

GLORIA: Well, I wouldn't even give you the satisfaction.

PERLS: Are you aware that your eyes are moist? You're smiling. You're smiling at something over there?

GLORIA: Well because I got two feelings, I was going to say, I want you to, I'd want you to love me and hug me, but then I thought no, I don't want that. I'd be scared to be too close to you.

PERLS: Now we're getting somewhere. Now we got the two poles of your existence. Either far away in a corner, or be so close that you get merged into one with the other person. It appears you travel between the two extremes. You cannot sustain contact.

SCENE 4
POST-THERAPY II

GLORIA: *(At mic.)* A frightened person does not smile.
Bullshit. All I wanted was permission to be me.

JANE: Maybe Gloria triggered something in him
inadvertently reminding him of his own parents who
rejected him. And then this happened.

*This happens as GLORIA describes it. PERLS watches her. He
catches her eye then cups his hand and beckons to her. She imitates
the gesture quizzically. It looks like a masturbation gesture. He
clarifies that he wants her to cup her hand. She does so and he
goes and tips his cigarette ash into her hand.*

GLORIA: After filming the weariness was apparent to
all of us. We were in the foyer, everybody smoking,
saying our goodbyes and thank yous. I noticed Dr Perls
scanning the room with his eyes. He made a motion
with his hands as if to say, 'Hold your hand in a cup-
like form – palm up.' Unconsciously I followed his
request – not really knowing what he meant. He flicked
his cigarette ash in my hand. Insignificant? Could be –
if one doesn't mind being mistaken for an ashtray.

GINA takes off PERLS' dick and puts it back in the drawer.

JANE: This from Fritz's autobiography concerning another
patient: 'I got her down again and said, gasping: "I've
beaten up more than one bitch in my life." Then she
got up, threw her arms around me: "Fritz, I love you."
Apparently she finally got what, all her life, she was

asking for, and there are thousands of women like her in the States. Provoking and tantalizing, bitching, irritating their husbands and never getting their spanking.'

GLORIA: What a jerk! I hated him for the rest of my life.

JANE sings and plays 'It's Obvious' by Au Pairs.

GINA on the couch. GLORIA behind, smoking.

SCENE 5
I REMEMBER

Five young women drift onto the stage as GINA *speaks.* JANE *plays 'In My Room' by The Beach Boys.*

GINA: I am so old now I remember when women had pubic hair.

The hair of her dickie-die-doh hung down to her knees – one black one, one white one and one with some shite on and the hair of her dickie-die-doh hung down to her knees.

I remember when poor people were thin.

I remember a sex education book called *My Dear Daughter.* It was read alone. There was no discussion about it. It referenced the Virgin Mary. Great help.

I remember at school we were warned not to accept a drink from men at a certain disco because they would put sperm into the bottle of Fanta and before you'd know it, you'd be up the duff. Fanta Fanta it's a bottle of cum.

I remember hearing the word masturbation for the first time. Masturbation. I was delighted it was a thing and not me being a freak but it sounded so masculine.

I remember my father's three pieces of advice to me – file your nails towards the centre, hang trousers seam to seam, and knee a man in the balls if he's bold. Not bad pointers coming from a violent alcoholic.

I remember seeing my father in a straightjacket.

I remember our mothers before divorce became legal calling marriage a life sentence.

I don't remember anyone ever talking to us as young women about enjoying sex. It was all avoidance and warnings. Something that was done to you. Nothing that you might willingly participate in unless you were a hoor, a doxy.

I remember ads for women's health clinics being blanked out of imported UK magazines.

I remember my mother's three pieces of advice to me – never trust blond men, don't go out with anyone better-looking than yourself, and to toughen.

I remember a neighbour telling us that on her wedding night her husband tried to enter her via her belly button.

I remember my friend's mother saying that she didn't know what a lesbian was until she was in her forties.

I remember getting my first period at a hypnotist's show. My friend got a leprechaun – equally mystifying and unexpected.

I remember being told I'd get what was coming to me because I was a prick-tease.

JANE sings.

I remember my friend scrubbing her vulva with a Brillo Pad after her brothers abused her.

I remember her mother crossing the courtroom to side with the brothers – though she knew.

I remember the farmer who wouldn't allow his wife to travel in his car. He made her stand in the trailer with the pigs instead.

I remember the hope of the '70s women's movement.

I remember not wearing a bra. The liberation.

I remember the punk who said *I want to lick your slit.*

I remember having underarm hair. A guy said it looked like I was carrying two mink.

I remember being in love, feeling equal.

I remember having a miscarriage during a game of Scrabble and saying I had an upset tummy, to count me out. I was losing anyway.

I remember the gynaecologist smoking and not wearing gloves.

I remember everybody's mother being tranked to the gills – a cure for monogamy. Tranks for the memories.

I remember two-timing – exhausting.

I remember thinking we could stop porn. Hah.

I remember the drunk guy in the waiting room at the STD clinic shouting *Yiz are all riddled.*

I remember being hit, once.

JANE sings.

I remember the mayhem of menopausal desire when you'd fuck anything, anyone. A traffic cone.

I remember not being able to buy tampons in China.

I remember being able to finally spend my abortion fund at menopause. It wasn't used for a trip to England.

I remember a friend saying somebody thought I was hot. Hot? Who, as an adult, wants to be described as hot? It just means fuckable on someone else's terms. I'm grand for hot, thanks.

I remember when the idea of Ireland being described as liberal was a joke.

I remember when truth had consequences.

I remember when IRL stood for Ireland, not In Real Life.

JANE sings.

Part III

SCENE 1

GINA, LIV, JANE and young women listen to SHOSTROM.

SHOSTROM: *(Voiceover.)* We're nearing the end of our therapeutic journey. You've visited with Dr Carl Rogers and with Dr Perls as they each have attempted to help Gloria with her personal concerns. Now we conclude with Dr Albert Ellis.

GINA gets the box with the drone dick.

GINA: And so to Dr Ellis's dick. Crescendo cock. This just keeps on giving, huh? It represents a huge part of the budget. We had a lot of explaining to do with our funders. Taxpayers' money, dear oh dear, being spent on chalky gonads. Honestly though, who wouldn't want to fuck the patriarchy. Took ages to work out the aerodynamics but I'm pretty sure I can get it up.

SHOSTROM: *(Voiceover.)* Dr Ellis is the founder of Rational Emotive Therapy.

JANE: And author of such classics as: *Nymphomania: A Study of the Oversexed Woman*; *How to Live with a Neurotic*; *Homosexuality: Its Causes and Cure*; and *The Intelligent Woman's Guide to Man-Hunting*.

GLORIA: By then I was tired, naturally, but I sure as hell perked up when I met him on set. He really was quite attractive. I mean, by comparison.

ELLIS: Rational Emotive Therapy is based on several fundamental propositions or hypotheses. The first of these is, the past is not crucial in a person's life. The past affects him but he affects himself much more than the past affects him. The only reason why things that happened during his historical development affect him today is because he's still re-indoctrinating himself with the same philosophies of life, the same values, that he taught himself too early in his childhood. And that's why he's disturbed.

AV title: 'Therapy Session 3'.

ELLIS in the therapist chair with the drone dick on the floor. GLORIA is relating events from her mic at the table, or has roving mic.

ELLIS: Hello Gloria, I'm Dr Ellis.

GLORIA: Hello Doctor! We shook hands. His palm was moist. It sort of sounded like a kiss. It actually made me feel a little horny. He knew it too. I could see it in his eyes. You know the kind of thing…there was a frisson, as the Frenchies say. He saw right through my dress.

JANE: His reputation preceded him. Rumour had it that he slept will all his female patients. Painfully shy as a youngster, he set out to change his behaviour and forced himself to speak to every woman he encountered at a park bench near his home. Over a month, he spoke to one hundred and thirty women and even managed to get one date. But he had desensitized himself and was no longer afraid of women.

GLORIA: Perspiration prickled in my armpits. My upper lip was glistening. I used to find that sort of intelligence so attractive. Couldn't help myself. That's what I was searching for. Smart sexy. I fumbled for my cigarettes. I wanted to disappear into my purse. That always happened to me with 'superior' kind of guys. I turned into this sort of ikky girl just giving them the stinky part of me. Oh, I missed a bunch of what he was saying then because he was making a vagina shape with his hands. Over his crotch. Jeez Louise. I could see the outline of his dick right through his pants. Framed by his hands!

ELLIS: What's at stake here is your shyness. It's just a small part of you. You're re-indoctrinating yourself with this negative self-def–

GLORIA: He was so close I could smell his breath. Even now I can still smell it. Aniseed-y. I was afraid the microphone would pick up my heart beating furiously. Boom boom. Boom boom. Boom boom. I, I, I was wet in all the wrong places. You know what I mean. I was the poster girl for desire alright. Telling him what I found attractive in a man made it worse. Other than his brain, I mean. I don't remember if I said neck? Maybe I did. The nape of the neck. Oh. Men in cars – trying to keep their eyes on the driving, their hands on the wheel. Those were the things that turned me on back then. To be honest, I could have climbed right on top of him. Is that so bad? He was really encouraging me to overcome my shyness around men like him, to take the risk of being me. To just…

ELLIS: …he rejects you but you don't have to reject you. Say you had a mangled arm. And you wouldn't accept the good parts of you because of this mangled arm. You're letting the bad bit of you be all of you. All you see is manglement. And it is mangled. Defective. Let's not pretend otherwise…

GLORIA: Yes, I said, when I could get a word in. I'd like to…but you know I realised he was more concerned with pushing his line in therapy than actually helping me. He went on and on with his hypotheses about fantasies of satisfaction being attacks on desire. He hardly paused for breath.

ELLIS: If you were my patient I'd give you a homework assignment. I'd send you out to get into trouble. Bad trouble. Leave that mangled arm at home.

GLORIA: Really doctor, I said, you mean go out to a bar or dancing? And he said…

ELLIS: Or go into a doctor's office…

GLORIA: I was incredulous. I said, 'You mean march right in there?'

ELLIS: Yeah, sure, if he's smart, an eligible individual and you find him attractive. Be brazen, Gloria. That's what you're saying you want. Stop thinking you're so special. What's stopping you?

GLORIA: What was he suggesting? That I go out and beg men to sleep with me? That I even ask him, straight out? Seriously.

ELLIS: Force yourself. Go for it, Gloria. Be bold. What you gotta lose, Gloria? Go get what you want. Force yourself to open your big mouth…

The drone dick flies over the stage. GLORIA beckons it and lands it in her hand.

GLORIA: I had had it up to here with him, his talking, his therapy and his cockamamie dick.

GINA: Jesus, what a relief. I'm glad I just have an X and Y in my name and not in my pants. Hashtag 'not all men'. I know. I know. It's the system. Here, let me deal with that. I'll just put this lad, this teaching tool, back in his box.

SHOSTROM: *(Voiceover.)* We hope that this journey into the private world of Gloria has been interesting and profitable.

GINA: Ah yeah, profitable for some. Actually, I'll just leave this shrivelled, white dick here so we can keep an eye on it. Don't trust what they get up to together behind closed drawers. Before you know it they're legislating their way into our uteruses.

SHOSTROM: *(Voiceover.)* We wish to express our gratitude to Gloria, the patient, and to her therapists for allowing us to share their therapeutic adventure.

GINA: Gloria was told that these films would be used for educational purposes in a classroom context so was fairly surprised a year or so later to see her interview with Dr Perls on TV and then to learn that the films were going to be shown in full in cinemas.

JANE: By then they were no longer even called *Three Approaches to Psychotherapy* but *The Gloria Films.* She began proceedings to sue Shostrom but got nowhere with the case.

GINA: I bashed into an old pal recently who had become a psychotherapist since we last met. He used to be an arts administrator. And guess what? He's actually making a living, but that's not the extraordinary bit. He told me they're still using the *Gloria Films* to train the up-and-coming therapists. I mean, for fuck's sake…will we ever get anywhere?

GINA moves to the couch with the young women. GLORIA to the therapist's chair.

SHOSTROM: *(Voiceover.)* Gloria, you've been through the mill today, haven't you?

You've been very courageous, willing to take risks,
and we're very grateful…

GLORIA: Don't you worry about me. I'll just be a footnote
for some Psych students. A curiosity on YouTube. Oh
sure the films went public without my permission but
what the heck, will that matter anymore? How many
times did she cross her legs? Who cares how much
I spoke. Did she have an affair with Rogers? No, it
was Ellis she had the affair with. Didn't she live with
Perls? Wasn't she a nymphomaniac? Didn't she die
by suicide? She was definitely lesbian. As I always say
believe half of what you see and none of what you hear.
Way in the future during the third wave of feminism
somebody will make a show about me. And there will
be waves after that and many more dicks to deal with
but the tide will turn. Can you feel it? Can you smell it?
Can you hear it? Yeah. There's no stopping it. Those
dominant and domineering structures will have to be
dealt with one by one. It's gonna get ugly. I'm getting
all fired up here. And you glorious creatures – you
be you. Doo beee dooo. You've got work to do. Keep
pushing. Don't be afraid. Embrace your desire. Love
yourself. Your body. Whoever you want. And love that
wanting. Yeah. Be bold. Be brazen. Be brave. Have
fun. Have sex. Have as much as you want. One small
favour – it's always really, really bugged me that the G
spot was named after a man, a German gynaecologist
called Gräfenberg. Is that a passion killer or what? Like
he fearlessly clambered into that vast luscious cavern
with his ice pick and crampons and heroically planted

his name at the very locus of female desire. Get out of there Gräfenberg. And all the other guys who planted their names in the innermost parts of us. I'm talking to you Gabrielis Fallopious. Let's put some real sexiness in there, starting with the G spot. Humour me. I'm changing things here. I'm making myself horny. Yeah. Hit that spot as often as you can. And call it what it is: Gloria. The Gloria spot. It's not so easy to find in there but let me tell you it is so explosively sweet even the trying is worth it. Let that be your homework from me. Hit that G spot and sing out GLORIA.

JANE plays 'Gloria' by Van Morrison. She and GLORIA sing.

GLORIA: You got that? GLORIA. That's right. Sing it. G-L-O-R-I-A. Call it GLORIA.

GINA and the young women come forward during GLORIA's speech and chime in on the GLORIA singing. Final instrumental. Strobe effect. The stage clears in blackout except for GINA. Spotlight on GINA.

GINA: Can you see me now?

Blackout.

The End.